MATTHEW'S LIFE OF CHRIST

Coordinated with the Other Three Gospels

EASY BIBLE SURVEY WORKBOOK

#3

Katheryn Maddox Haddad

Other Books by this Author

BIBLICAL HISTORICAL NOVELS
Series of 8: Soul Journey With the Real Jesus
Ongoing Series of 8: Intrepid Men of God

CHILDREN'S BIBLE STORYBOOKS
Series of 8: A Child's Life of Christ
Series of 10: A Child's Bible Heroes
Series of 8: A Child's Bible Kids

WORLDWIDE HISTORICAL RESEARCH
DOCUMENTARY, THESIS, NOVEL & SCREENPLAY WRITERS

BIBLE TOPICS
Applied Christianity: Handbook 500 Good Works
Christianity or Islam? The Contrast
The Holy Spirit: 592 Verses Examined
Inside the Hearts of Bible Women-Reader+Audio+Leader
Revelation: A Love Letter From God
Worship Changes Since 1st Century + Worship 1st Century Way
Was Jesus God? (Why Evil)
365 Life-Changing Scriptures Day by Date
The Road to Heaven
The Lord's Supper: 52 Readings with Prayers

BIBLE FUN BOOKS
Bible Puzzles, Bible Song Book, Bible Numbers

TOUCHING GOD SERIES
365 Golden Bible Thoughts: God's Heart to Yours
365 Pearls of Wisdom: God's Soul to Yours
365 Silver-Winged Prayers: Your Spirit to God's

SURVEY SERIES: EASY BIBLE WORKBOOKS
→Old Testament & New Testament Surveys
→Questions You Have Asked-Part I & II

Genealogy: How to Climb Your Family Tree Without Falling Out
Volume I & 2: Beginner-Intermediate & Colonial-Medieval

COVER BY SHARON LAVY
Copyright © 2014 Katheryn Maddox Haddad   ISBN-978-1-952261-46-6
NORTHERN LIGHTS PUBLISHING HOUSE
All rights reserved. May not be printed in any form without permission.

Contents

Other Books by this Author..ii
How to Use This Book..5

Week One
   Introduction 7
  Ch 1   Jesus' Ancestry and Birth...7
  Ch 2   Jesus' Early Childhood..9
  Ch 3   John the Baptist 11
  Ch 4   Jesus' Temptation and First Apostles 13

Week Two
  Ch 5   Sermon on the Mount I...16
  Ch 6   Sermon on the Mount II..18
  Ch 7   Sermon on the Mount III...19
  Ch 8   Jesus' First Healings 21

Week Three
  Ch 8   Jesus' First Healing...24
  Ch 9   Jesus Recruits Matthew 26
  Ch 10   Jesus Selects & Assigns 12 Apostles 28
  Ch 11   John the Baptist 31

Week Four
  Ch 12 Jesus Faces His First Accusers 33
  Ch 13 Famous Parables 35
  Ch 14 John the Baptist Executed 38

Week Five
  Ch 15 Jesus Escapes to a Foreign Country 42
  Ch 16 Jesus Escapes to Another Foreign Country..........44
  Ch 17 Jesus' Body Transfigured/Transformed 46
  Ch 18 Get Along With Others 48

Week Six

- Ch 19   Jesus Talks About Family 50
- Ch 20   Jesus' New Kingdom, the Church 52
- Ch 21   Triumphant Entry Into Jerusalem 54

Week Seven
- Ch 22   Jesus' Showdown With Religious Hierarchy 59
- Ch 23   Jesus Condemns Hypocrite Religious Leaders ... 61
- Ch 24   Jesus Predicts the Beginning of the Church 64

Week Eight
- Ch 25   Parables & Parallels 68
- Ch 26   Introduces Lord's Supper, then Agonizes 69
- Ch 27   The Crucifixion 74
- Ch 28   Jesus' Resurrection and Great Commission 79

A Few of Many Predictions Jesus Fulfilled in His Life 82

Thank You 83
About The Author 84
Connect With the Author 85
Buy Your Next Book Now 86

How to Use This Book

Dear Bible Student:

The Bible is easy to understand. It is people who make it complicated. These lessons are surveys, not in-depth studies.

Despite good intentions, many people in our fast-paced world today find it difficult to find time to learn the Bible. If you are one of these, this book is for you. You will be in and out of the study in no time.

The Bible has been translated into English several times. I suggest, if you do not have one, you order a New International Version (NIV) since many of the questions are fill-in-the-blank. NIVs are sold everywhere.

Dates are based on the corrected Gregorian Calendar. Therefore, Jesus was born 6 BC, two or four years before King Herod died.

The questions are easy. They go right down the line, verse by verse. Each week is subdivided into days, so you need not spend more than about ten minutes a day learning. Remember, your best learning is done when you are studying alone.

You may decide to make this a group study. Since you have already looked up all the verses in your Bible at home, it is suggested that you go through all the answers in a timely and lively manner.

But do take your Bible with you to your study group. Sometimes we misread a verse and get a wrong answer (in a hurry that day?), so those are the verses you will want to look up when together with your study group.

For further ease in study, your group leader may wish to supply you with a list of page numbers a week ahead of time for the few scriptures referred to in other parts of the Bible. If you prefer to use a Bible you already have, put a bookmark in the Table of Contents of your Bible. Most Tables of Contents are both in alphabetical order and chronological order.

Try to set aside an hour and a half for your study group. Spend your first half hour sharing your past week with each other, followed by a prayer for each other. You can go through all the questions allotted for each week in the remaining hour.

Matthew's Life of Christ

Should questions arise requiring more in-depth study, write them down. Then, at the end of your eight- or ten-week study, set aside a month for them. Use a concordance or word search and look up everything the Bible has to say about that subject. That is easy to do.

I guarantee that you will learn so much in just one week that you will be thrilled. Many people using these lessons say they learn more in one week than they do in a year normally. I hope this does not describe your past, but if it does, tell yourself, "And this is just the beginning!"

Should you have a question, contact me through my website at **https://NorthernLightsPublishingHouse.com**

Coordinated With the Other Three Gospels

Week One

DAY ONE:

Introduction

The Bible is divided into two parts. The Old Testament is everything from the creation to the birth of Jesus, and covers approximately 4000 years. The New Testament is everything from the birth of Jesus Christ to the death of the last apostle nearly 100 years later.

Within the Bible are 66 smaller books usually named after a main event in it, the author, or to whom it was written. Four men wrote the life of Christ. Matthew was a Jew and one of the 12 apostles of Jesus. Mark was a companion of the apostle Peter. Luke was a Greek physician and companion of the apostle Paul. John was a Jew and one of the 12 apostles of Jesus. Although all four accounts are similar, some include facts that the others do not.

The land of Israel was divided into three parts. In the south, where Jerusalem was, was the province of Judea; in the middle, where some half-breed Jews lived, was the province of Samaria, and in the north, where Jesus grew up, was the province of Galilee.

Matthew Chapter 1
BC 7 ~ Jesus' Ancestry and Birth

VERSE 1
The human part of Jesus was a direct descendant of the Father of the Jewish (Israelite) Nation, whose name was _____ _____ (Hint: See Romans 11:1,)

VERSE 2
Jesus descended through Abraham's grandson, named _____ (This grandson had so many children, instead of calling it a family, his descendants were called a tribe.)

VERSE 5
One of Jesus' female ancestors was _____.
It was her vow that is repeated today at weddings sometimes:

"Entreat me not to leave thee

Matthew's Life of Christ

> *or to return from following after thee:*
> *for whither thou goest, I will go;*
> *and where thou lodgest, I will lodge:*
> *thy people shall be my people,*
> *and thy God my God."*

VERSE 6
The first king in Jesus' ancestry was King _____

VERSE 7
The next king in Jesus' ancestry, Solomon, was known worldwide for what? (See Matthew 12:42). _____

VERSE 18
_____ was a virgin pledged to be married to Joseph. (See also Luke 1:26-31). Jesus was born of a human mother, but the divine part of Jesus was a descendent of _____ (see Luke 1:32-35).

NOTE: When the Holy Spirit "overshadowed" Mary so that she became pregnant, it is the same word used when the Holy Spirit "hovered" over a formless, dark, and void mass at the birth of our world. (See Genesis 1:2-3)

VERSE 19
In Bible times, to be engaged was as legally binding as today's marriages. That is why Joseph decided to _____

NOTE: From what we can tell, he knew Mary was pregnant, and he was not the father. According to Jewish law, someone could be divorced for adultery. Apparently, Joseph thought Mary had committed adultery.

Worse, the woman could be stoned to death in front of her parents' house. (Deuteronomy 21:22 in the Old Testament). The penalty was harsh because sexual sins are horrifying in the eyes of God. Such penalties served as deterrents.

DAY TWO:

VERSE 20

Coordinated With the Other Three Gospels

Who came to set Joseph straight on how Mary became pregnant?
_____

VERSE 21
What does the name Jesus mean? (See the footnote in your Bible.)
_____

VERSE 23
According to the footnote in your Bible, what prophet, who lived 700 years earlier, prophesied that Jesus' mother would be a virgin? _____ (His writings are found in the Old Testament.)

What does the word E-mman-u-El mean? _____
_____

VERSE 25
Joseph did not have marital relations with Mary until when?
_____

Does this show she did or did not remain a virgin the rest of their marriage? _____

When Jesus was born, he was laid in an animal's _____ (See Luke 2:7).

The angels appeared to the shepherds the same _____ (See Luke 2:11)

Matthew Chapter 2
BC 6-AD 6 ~ Jesus' Early Childhood

VERSE 1
Jesus was born in what town and province? _____
_____

Who was the king of the Jews at this time? _____

How many Magi (wise men) arrived from "the east?" _____

NOTE: This is a trick question.

Matthew's Life of Christ

VERSE 2
While they were still in the east, they saw his _____

NOTE: 600 years earlier, a Jew lived living in "the east" named Daniel became the Prime Minister of that area (Persia). He left behind writings which predicted the exact year the King of Kings would begin to reign, and other Jewish writings which predicted this king would be a Jew represented by a star.

VERSE 3
What man and what city were disturbed when they heard a new king had been born? _____

NOTE: Herod was a half-Jew, half-Arab appointed by Caesar to be king over the Jews. When he took over the country, the Jews slammed the gates of Jerusalem shut and wouldn't let him in. So he had to storm the city, killing 12,000 Jews in the process, many of them in the Temple itself. (See *Josephus*, noted Jewish historian of the first century AD.)

DAY THREE:

VERSE 4
Who did King Herod call together to find out where Jesus was to be born? _____ and _____

VERSE 5
How did they know Jesus would be born in Bethlehem? _____
_____

VERSE 9-10
The _____ which they had seen while in the east (Persia, Iraq, India probably) reappeared to lead them to where Jesus was.

VERSE 11
By this time, Mary, Joseph, and Jesus were living in a _____

What gifts did they present to Jesus? _____
_____

VERSE 13

Coordinated With the Other Three Gospels

For a second time, God appeared to Joseph. This time he warned him to escape who what country? _____

VERSE 16
King Herod had already killed his wife, his mother-in-law, his grandfather-in-law, his brother-in-law, and three sons because he thought they were trying to take over his throne (Josephus). So now Herod ordered all boys _____ years old and under to be killed.

NOTE: If the wise men lived in Persia 1000 miles away, it might have taken them a year to figure out from the Jewish writings in their archives (left there by Daniel) what the star meant, and another year to travel to Jerusalem.

VERSE 22
They were in Egypt until Herod died two years later. For a third time, God appeared to Joseph to warn him not to settle in the Province of _____ where Herod's cruel son, Archelaeus was made governor. So Joseph went to which province that was governed by a better son of Herod? _____

VERSE 23
What town did Jesus grow up in? _____
This was located in the province of Galilee, far north of the Province of Judea, where Jerusalem and the Temple were.

Matthew Chapter 3
AD 27 ~ John the Baptist

DAY FOUR:

VERSE 1-2
Who told people to repent? _____
_____ Why?
_____
_____

What is another word for kingdom that was used after it came? (Hint: Compare Acts 20:28 with Revelation 1:5b-6) _____
_____

Matthew's Life of Christ

VERSE 6
People who repented did what in the Jordan River?
_____

VERSE 7
The Pharisees (pronounced fair-a-sees) and Sadducees (pronounced sad-u-cees) were denominations within the Jewish religion. The Pharisees believed that, after you died, God raised you back to life again to dwell with him. The Sadducees believed that once you died, you were like Rover - dead all over.

Whenever John or Jesus talked about or to the Pharisees, it was to their leaders. For instance, when we talk about a political party, we are referring to its leaders.

VERSE 9
These Jewish leaders were bragging that who was their ancestor?
_____

VERSE 10-12
Baptism by the Holy Spirit meant that, at baptism, we receive _____ of our sins and the gift of _____ _____ (see Acts 2:38).

Baptism of fire is explained in the Apostle Paul's letter to the church in Corinth, 1 Corinthians 3:13. What is it? _____
_____
_____

VERSE 13-15
Jesus insisted on being baptized so he could fulfill all _____ _____ as an example to us.

VERSE 16
Jesus came _____ _____ of the water.
That means his baptism involved him going down into the water. Would he have needed to do this if baptism was sprinkling?
_____

VERSE 16-17
This was the first time the three parts of God were revealed. God's

Coordinated With the Other Three Gospels

_____ _____ descended in the form of a dove and the voice was God the Father bragging on his _____ whom he loved.

Was God happy or angry that Jesus had been baptized?_____
So, when you are baptized, is God happy, sad, or doesn't really care?

Matthew Chapter 4
Jesus' Temptation and First Apostles

DAY FIVE:

VERSE 1
Jesus was tempted by whom?

_____

VERSE 2
Jesus fasted how long? _____

VERSE 3
The devil said he would believe Jesus was the Son of God IF he performed what kind of miracle for Jesus's own benefit?

_____

Even if Satan had believed Jesus was the Son of God, would he have been saved? Does belief/faith alone save a person? (Hint: See James 2:17 & 19)? _____

NOTE: If Jesus had done what Satan said, who would he be obeying? _____

VERSE 4
Jesus fought Satan by quoting from the Bible, an Old Testament scripture written by Moses about 2500 B.C., saying that true life is given by words from the _____

VERSE 5-6

Matthew's Life of Christ

So Satan quoted scripture (Psalm 91:11-12) as part of his next dare. He dared Jesus to perform another miracle on his own behalf by jumping off the pinnacle of the _____.
Can you conclude from this that not everyone who quotes the Bible is saved? _____

VERSE 7
Jesus again replied by quoting another scripture written by Moses saying we should not put God to the _____

Do people sometimes put themselves in dangerous situations and then get mad at God for not getting them out of it? _____
_____

If Jesus had jumped, who would he have been obeying? _____

VERSE 10
Finally, Satan admitted his ulterior motives: Worship me. Jesus answered with another scripture, this time one of the Ten Commandments written by Moses, "Worship _____
only.

DAY SIX:

VERSE 11
Only after resisting several times did the devil _____
Jesus. Then God sent his _____ to take care of Jesus' needs.

VERSE 13
Jesus grew up in Nazareth. But at this time he moved to Capernaum (pronounced Cap-er-nium) by a large _____
sometimes called a sea.

VERSE 17
Jesus then began preaching the same message as John, that people should _____. Acknowledging that we sin is the first step to turning to God and his help. There are three kinds of sins: (1) Bad we do, (2) Bad we think, (3) Good we do not do.

Jesus was how old when he began preaching? See Luke 3:23. ___

Coordinated With the Other Three Gospels

VERSE 18
What was the name of the large lake? _____
What two fishermen did he call to join him? _____
and _____

VERSE 19
What did he say they would fish for from then on? _____

VERSE 21
What other two brothers - also fishermen - did he call next?
_____ and _____

VERSE 23
Jesus preached in synagogues (pronounced sin-a-gogs) and proved his message was from God by healing _____ disease and sickness.

Notice, he never failed to heal a person, and it was always instant.

VERSE 24
News about Jesus also spread to what country just north of Palestine? _____

VERSE 25
Galilee was the northern province of Palestine/Israel. The southern province was Judea where Jerusalem was located, the middle province was Samaria, and a fourth province was on the east side of the Jordan River called Perea. (Decapolis refers to a metropolitan area in Galilee made up of ten cities.)

Matthew's Life of Christ

Week Two

Matthew Chapter 5
Sermon on the Mount

DAY ONE:

VERSE 3
We must admit that we are impoverished spiritually and need God because of our _____ nature before we can have the kingdom of heaven.

VERSE 4
Once we recognize our spiritual poverty, we _____ for our sins. Only then can God comfort us.

VERSE 5
It has been said that meekness is not being self-serving. In what way would meek people feel as though all the true riches of the earth belonged to them? _____
_____

VERSE 6
Once we realize how spiritually poor we are and mourn over it and become meek, we will realize how _____ and _____ we are for righteousness.

VERSE 7
Once we admit our sins to God, we can be _____ to other people who sin.

VERSE 8
To be pure means to be all one thing—pure gold, pure cotton, etc. with no impurities. If our hearts are pure in the above things, our hearts will be like pure glass. Then we will be able to _____
_____ for what he truly is.

VERSE 9
Then we will want to become _____

Coordinated With the Other Three Gospels

between man and man, and between God and man. When we do that, we are acting like Jesus and are called _____ of God.

VERSE 10
What is one way to know we are succeeding in being like Jesus? Being _____ by people who do not want to be like him.

DAY TWO:

VERSE 13
Salt is used to preserve things. In this sense, how can Christians be salt to people around them? _____
_____

VERSE 16
What in our lives makes us light to others? _____
_____

VERSE 17-20
Jesus is the only one to have ever lived the Law of Moses (in the Old
Testament) perfectly, and never sin (see Hebrews 4:15). On the cross, the last thing Jesus said was (John 19:30) _____
_____

NOTE: Hebrews 9:15 says Jesus did away with the Old Will and Testament of God and put into effect a New Will and Testament when he died on the cross. That is why Christians obey the New Testament, the last half of the Bible. We are not bound by the Old Testament Law of Moses, the first part of the Bible.

VERSE 21-22
Jesus said we can be guilty of _____
in the eyes of God just by being _____
with his brother.

VERSE 23-24
Before God blesses our offerings at church, we need to try to be_____ with people who are offended by us.

VERSE 27
Jesus said we can be guilty of _____ in the eyes of God just by _____ at a woman [or man] lustfully.

DAY THREE:

VERSE 31
Jesus said we should divorce only for marital _____

VERSE 33-37
People should trust our word so much that they believe it when we say _____ or _____

VERSE 38-42
Jesus said we were not to follow the old adage "Eye for eye, and _____ for _____ as found in the Law of Moses, but rather not even resist those who harm us. Is this easy to do? _____

VERSE 43-44
Jesus said we were to love who? Our _____
Is this easy to do? _____

VERSE 46-47
By being good to those who are bad to us, we reveal God to them. What is God? (Hint, see 1 John 4:16). _____

Matthew Chapter 6
Sermon on the Mount

VERSE 1
If we do good works and make sure others know about it, we will have no _____ from God.

VERSE 7
Our prayers should not be _____, (AKA vain repetitions) saying the same phrase over and over or reciting a section of a holy book over and over.

Coordinated With the Other Three Gospels

VERSE 9-13
This is the "Lord's Prayer." It consists of the following categories, which we can use in our own prayers:

    a. Praise to God
    b. Willingness for God's will to be done
    c. Request for basic essentials of life
    d. Request for forgiveness
    e. Request for strength to resist Satan

VERSE 16-18
Jesus assumed we would fast, for he said _____ you fast, not IF you fast.

VERSE 19-21
How can we store up treasures in heaven? (Hint: See Paul's first letter to Timothy, chapter 6, verses 18 and 19)
_____
_____

DAY FOUR

VERSE 22-23
To have eyes that do not see (see Matthew 13:14) can mean that people in Jesus' day saw him as a man, but never saw him as the Son of _____

VERSE 24-34
Jesus tells us not to _____ especially about what is going to happen _____.

Matthew Chapter 7
Sermon on the Mount

VERSE 1-5
Jesus said here not to judge, but in John 7:24 he said we were not to judge by _____ appearance, indicating that what Jesus is talking about in Matthew is not to be judgmental.

VERSE 6

Matthew's Life of Christ

Jesus said we need to judge if we are wasting our time trying to explain God to people who do not want to hear it. Doing that is like throwing _____ to swine.

VERSE 7
"_____ and it will be _____ to you." Just a few minutes earlier, Jesus had said not to worry about such things as _____, but to seek what first? _____
_____
James 4:3 says we ask with the wrong _____ so we can have more to spend on our own _____. Prayer is not a blank check for anything we want.

VERSE 8
What is behind the door he wants us to knock on (see Revelation 3:20)? _____

VERSE 12
Jesus summarized the entire Old Testament and its 600 laws with this single sentence: Do to _____
_____
This is also called the "golden rule."

VERSE 13
Jesus is considered by many to be "narrow-minded" because he said the only way to eternal life is through him. This is stated in John 3:16, which says _____
_____
_____

DAY FIVE

VERSE 14
Does God want anyone to be lost? See the second letter that Peter wrote, chapter 3, verse 9. _____

VERSE 15
Jesus predicted there would be _____

Coordinated With the Other Three Gospels

_____. In the Greek language in which the New Testament was written, "prophet" merely meant teacher, not someone who foretold the future (although sometimes they did).

VERSE 16-20
If a false prophet told people they could become Christians by walking ten miles backward, would they be producing Christians in God's sight? _____

VERSE 21
Jesus said it is not enough just to call him _____.
That alone does not guarantee someone is a Christian and saved.

VERSE 22-23
Jesus said some would even perform _____ in his name, but he will deny even knowing them.

VERSE 24-27
Jesus wants people to hear his _____ and put them into _____ He will consider these people _____. People who hear him but refuse to do what he said he calls what? _____

Matthew Chapter 8
AD 28 ~ Jesus' First Healings

VERSE 1-4
In light of what Jesus was just preaching about, why do you think Jesus told the leper he had healed not to tell anyone?

_____

NOTE: In the Old Testament, the Law of Moses said that, when someone recovered from a disease, they were to go to a priest who acted as a health officer. If the priest pronounced him fully recovered, he then offered a sacrifice to God. That's why Jesus told the healed man to show himself to a priest. Jesus obeyed the Old Testament Law of Moses perfectly – the only person to ever do so.

VERSE 5
A century means 100 years; therefore, a Roman centurion is a

Matthew's Life of Christ

commander in charge of how many soldiers? _____

DAY SIX

VERSE 6
The centurion's _____ was _____
and in _____ suffering.

VERSE 10
Why was Jesus astonished that this foreigner so readily believed in him? _____

VERSE 11
Jesus then condemned the lack of faith of the Jews by saying foreigners will come from the _____
(Orient?) and the west (the Americas?) to join the founders of the Jewish faith in the

_____

VERSE 12
Then, not only will there be foreigners in the kingdom of heaven, but those who most expected to be there, the _____
will be thrown out. Why will they be thrown out (look again at the end of verse 10)?

_____

NOTE: For 2500 years, the Old Testament had predicted everything about Jesus' life, even when he would be born, where he would be born, where he would grow up, and so on. No other nationality had access to these O.T. scriptures. But, with all these advantages, the Jews still would not believe Jesus was the Savior that had been predicted.

VERSE 13
When was the centurion's servant healed? _____

_____

VERSE 14
Was Peter ever married? _____

VERSE 15
What did his mother-in-law do after Jesus healed her? _____

Coordinated With the Other Three Gospels

VERSE 17
Seven centuries earlier, Isaiah predicted that the savior would take our _____ and carry our

Matthew's Life of Christ

Week Three

Matthew Chapter 8 (continued)
Jesus' First Healing

DAY ONE:

VERSE 18-19
Jesus tried to escape a crowd by crossing to the other side of the _____
Some people, including a teacher, told him he would _____ him to the other side. This teacher bragged that he would _____ Jesus _____ _____ he went.

VERSE 20
But Jesus said, even though animals have homes, he did not have a _____ to lay his _____, probably meaning he did not own a place of his own and often slept in the open when traveling.

NOTE: Jesus called himself the Son of Man 88 times, and Ezekiel, an Old Testament prophet, was called a son of man by God over 90 times. In Ezekiel's case, God was telling Ezekiel he was a representative of mankind to mankind. He was a man, a son of mankind. As for Jesus, he was a son of mankind in the same way as Ezekiel. However, he was also God the Word with human flesh in a human body (See John 1:1 & 14 and Hebrews 10:5). He also acknowledged he was the Son of God (Luke 22:70).

So, why was Ezekiel called just **A** son of man, but Jesus called himself **THE** son of man? Jesus was also fulfilled the prophecy of Daniel when he saw a vision of "one like a son of man, coming with the clouds" ruling the world and being worshiped (Daniel 7:13-14) So, when the priests asked, "You are the Son of God, then?" (Mark 16:61-62), he replied yes and they would see him coming in the clouds. Jesus was not just A son of man, he was always THE Son of Man.

VERSE 21-22

Coordinated With the Other Three Gospels

Jesus took advantage of every situation to teach a lesson. When someone said they would follow Jesus as soon as they buried their _____, Jesus said let the _____ bury their own _____.
In what sense do you think he meant they were dead (see Colossians 2:13)? _____
_____

NOTE: People always buried their dead the same day they died. The man's father had not even died yet.

VERSE 23-24
What was Jesus doing in the boat during the storm while it was being swamped with water? _____

VERSE 25
His disciples shouted that they were about to do what?
_____
_____

VERSE 26-27
Jesus said they had little _____. He had just promised them in chapter 4, verse 19 they were going to live long enough to be _____ _____ They'd already forgotten his promise.

Then Jesus rebuked the _____ and the _____ , and the water became _____ Little by little he was revealing to his followers just who and what he was—the Creator.

VERSE 28
Once Jesus and his friends arrived on the other side of the _____ of Galilee, who came to meet him?_____
_____

VERSE 29
The demons knew right away that Jesus was the _____ of _____

Matthew's Life of Christ

They knew Jesus had the power to send them to torture, which was also called the Abyss (see Luke 8:31). Who is the "god" of the Abyss? Look at Revelation 9:1, 2, 11, and Luke 10:18.
_____

Who else is there (Jude 6)? _____

VERSE 30-32
Apparently, as long as demons can possess some living being on earth, they do not have to go to the Abyss. In the same way, humans resisted having demons in them, the pigs did too, even if it meant destroying themselves.

NOTE: We have no evidence that demons possessed anyone after Jesus' death. Jesus said several times just prior to his death IN John 12;31, "Now judgment is upon this world; now the ruler of this world will be _____."

Matthew Chapter 9
Jesus Recruits Matthew

DAY TWO:

VERSE 2
Not always, but Jesus recognized the fact that sometimes our own sins cause our illnesses. What are some sins that cause illnesses today? _____
_____
_____

VERSE 5-6
Jesus said he performed miracles in order to prove he had power to
_____

VERSE 2 & 6
Notice, Jesus first took care of the man's spiritual needs by doing what? _____ Secondly, he took care of the man's _____ needs.

VERSE 7
Thus far in our study, did Jesus ever fail to heal someone and then blame it on their lack of faith? _____

Coordinated With the Other Three Gospels

Do you recall one healing where the sick person had no faith at all because he did not know anything about his master asking Jesus to heal him? (Look back at chapter 8.) Who was his master?
_____

Thus far in our study, did Jesus ever partially heal someone and claim it was a healing anyway? _____

VERSE 9
What was Matthew's occupation? _____
_____. Do you think he was very popular? _____ Did Jesus seem to care whether or not he was popular? _____

Who is the author of the book we are reading? _____

VERSE 10
In Jesus' day, the religious people lumped what two groups of people together? _____ and
_____

VERSE 12
Jesus was not beyond using sarcasm to get his point across to hard-hearted people. What did he tell the self-righteous Pharisee religious leaders? _____
_____

VERSE 15
Jesus said that fasting was a sign of his _____
and _____ He said those associating with him need not fast until he, their _____, was taken from them. If he is the bridegroom, who is the bride (see Ephesians 5:25-33)? _____

VERSE 16-17
Jesus was bringing a new way of life. Instead of the Old Testament Law of Moses, which was impossible to keep, he was introducing a New Testament centered around the law of love. Do you think Jesus wants us to try to keep both the Old Testament Law of Moses and the New Testament Law of Christ? _____

Matthew's Life of Christ

(Think before you answer. If you want to bring back tithing, etc., you'll have to bring back stoning for adultery.)

DAY THREE

VERSE 18
When Mark told this same story, he said the ruler who came to Jesus ruled the local _____ (see Mark 5:22). His daughter had just _____.
Although Jesus had never done this before, he believed Jesus would bring her back to _____

VERSE 20
A woman interrupted Jesus because she had menstruated for _____ years.

VERSE 21
She believed Jesus would _____ her without even knowing it.

VERSE 25
To bring the girl back to life, did Jesus go into a long ceremony?
_____

VERSE 27-31
Sometimes Jesus healed people without them having faith (the dead girl had none), and sometimes he said _____ to their faith they would be healed.

VERSE 32-34
By what powers did the religious leaders from Jerusalem, the Jewish headquarters, claim Jesus cast out demons?
_____ Were they right? _____
Why do you think they told people this? _____
_____

Matthew Chapter 10
AD 29 - Jesus Selects & Assigns 12 Apostles
Then Warns Them of a Hard Life

VERSE 1-2

Coordinated With the Other Three Gospels

Jesus had twelve special disciples (meaning followers) which he now began to call his twelve _____
He personally gave them power to perform _____

VERSE 2-4
List the twelve apostles:

_____
_____
_____
_____
_____
_____

VERSE 5-7
Rather than have them go to all nationalities to start with, Jesus told them to go to the _____ sheep of _____ (the Jews).

DAY FOUR:

VERSE 8-11
Jesus told his apostles when they traveled to allow people who had received healing and heard their sermons to provide them a place to stay and food to eat because the _____ is worthy of his keep.

VERSE 15
Why were Sodom and Gomorrah so bad (2 Peter 2:6-7 & Jude 7)?
_____
What happened to Sodom and Gomorrah? _____
_____
But on the Day of Judgment, who will be dealt with more harshly?
_____

VERSE 16
Jesus told his apostles to be as _____ as snakes and _____ as doves.

VERSE 17-18
Jesus also warned them that all would not go well. Religious leaders would have them beaten right there in their _____ and political leaders would take them before _____

Matthew's Life of Christ

_____

VERSE 21
What will happen to families where some believe in Jesus, and others do not? _____

VERSE 24-25
Jesus was called _____, a name referring to the devil, by people who claimed he was casting out demons through the devil (remember 9:34?).

VERSE 28
Who are we to be the most afraid of? _____
What kind of people do you think can kill our souls? _____
_____

VERSE 32-33
If we acknowledge Jesus before men, Jesus will _____ us before _____

DAY FIVE

VERSE 34-35
Would families who split over their opinions of Jesus have been better off had Jesus never come in the first place? _____
_____
_____

VERSE 37
Do you think ultimately a marriage is worse off if they love God more than each other? (Consider 1 John 4:16) _____ Why?
_____

VERSE 38-39
If we die because of our belief in Jesus, what kind of life will we gain? _____

VERSE 42
If we give a _____ of _____ to anyone because we are Christians, Jesus will reward us.

Coordinated With the Other Three Gospels

Matthew Chapter 11
John the Baptist

VERSE 2
John the Baptist was now where? _____

VERSE 3-4
Even though he was a religious leader, he had honest problems with his faith. Did Jesus condemn him for it? _____

VERSE 5
Jesus helped John by reassuring him that he was fulfilling a prophecy about him from seven centuries earlier.

VERSE 7-8
Apparently those who had known John before thought he was awkward alike a reed _____ in the _____. He also apparently had been a man who dressed in _____.
But John had changed.

VERSE 10
Even John had fulfilled a prophecy about him made about 600 years earlier.

DAY SIX:

VERSE 11
Remembering that the kingdom of heaven is the church (above, chapter 3), the church began after Jesus returned to Heaven. John was beheaded shortly after this conversation with Jesus, why would someone in the kingdom/church be greater than John the Baptist? _____
_____

VERSE 18-19
John was condemned for abstaining from _____
_____ and Jesus was
condemned for _____
Does that sound like the way we judge people today? _____

VERSE 20

Matthew's Life of Christ

Even though Jesus performed numerous miracles in a certain few cities, he turned right around and condemned them because
_____

Do we today find it hard to identify our own sins? _____
Why? _____
_____

VERSE 22-23
Tyre and Sidon were Gentile cities in today's Lebanon. Yet, they will be judged more leniently than the very town Jesus was now living in, which was _____

VERSE 27
Why is it that we can only know the Father through the Son (see John 1:1-2 & 14)? _____
_____

VERSE 28
Jesus said, "_____ unto _____ , all you who are _____ and _____ and _____ will _____ you _____

VERSE 29
Take _____ yoke upon you and _____ from me, for I am _____ and _____ in _____, and _____ will find _____ for your _____.

VERSE 30
What is Jesus' yoke (see Philippians 1:1-2; 4:3) _____
_____
_____

What burden do we, in turn, put on Jesus (see Philippians 4:4-7)?
_____
_____

Coordinated With the Other Three Gospels

Week Four

Matthew Chapter 12
Jesus Faces His First Accusers

DAY ONE:

VERSE 1
On the _____ , Jesus' disciples began to pick some _____
and _____ them.

NOTE: According to the Law of Moses in the Old Testament, no one was to work on the Sabbath. However, if someone was traveling and hungry, they were allowed to pick enough to eat from anyone's field as long as they did not take any with them.

VERSE 2
The leaders of the Pharisee religious sect twisted the scriptures and said they couldn't do that on which day? _____

VERSE 3-4
But Jesus reminded them how _____ ate the _____ that was in the tabernacle when he was hungry.

VERSE 14
After Jesus healed the man's shriveled hand, the Pharisees plotted to _____ Jesus. Why do you think the religious leaders hated Jesus so much? _____
_____

VERSE 15
Knowing his teaching work was not done yet, Jesus _____ from that place.

VERSE 16
Once more, Jesus warned those he healed not to_____
_____ _____ Why do you think he told them this? _____
_____

Matthew's Life of Christ

VERSE 18
Jesus was fulfilling a prophecy about him given by Isaiah 700 years earlier: He will proclaim _____
_____ _____

VERSE 19
He will not _____

VERSE 20
He will be so kind, he won't even break a _____
What a contrast to the religious leaders trying to kill him!

DAY TWO:

VERSE 22
In an effort to trap him, the religious leaders brought him a
_____man.

VERSE 23
The people were gradually coming to realize that perhaps Jesus was the predicted _____

VERSE 26
Jesus said, "If _____ drives out _____, he will destroy himself.

VERSE 28
He made them face the fact that there was only one logical explanation, and that was that he drove out demons by the
_____ .

VERSE 30
We cannot straddle the fence. Jesus said, "He who is not
_____ me is _____ me."

VERSE 31-32
Anyone who speaks against the _____
_____ will not be forgiven.

NOTE: John 16:13 says the Holy Spirit will _____
_____ us into all _____.

Coordinated With the Other Three Gospels

Therefore, to reject the Holy Spirit is to reject Truth. John 16:8 says the Counselor (Holy Spirit) will _____ the world of _____. It is impossible for God to forgive someone who does not think they have any sins.

VERSE 36
On the Day of Judgment, we will give an _____ for every _____ we have _____

VERSE 37
Ultimately, it will be our _____ that condemn or acquit us, not an arbitrary whim of God.

VERSE 38
Jesus had already performed numerous miracles. Yet the Pharisees demand to see a _____

DAY THREE:

VERSE 40
In what way would Jesus be underground for three days (see Matthew 16:21)? _____

VERSE 41
Jesus praised the city of _____ , even though they were Gentiles and trying to conquer Israel, because when _____ preached to them, they repented.

VERSE 46-50
Taking advantage of every opportunity to teach a lesson, Jesus said the whole crowd was his _____ and _____

Matthew Chapter 13
A Chapter of Parables

(See below for coverage of verses 1-9)

VERSE 13
In what way does this verse sometimes apply to us today when we read God's word? _____

Matthew's Life of Christ

_____

VERSE 15
People's _____ become _____
It is almost as if, when we refuse to understand and accept the obvious in the Bible, we do not want Jesus to _____
_____ us (forgive us).

VERSE 18
The seed in the parable represents what (verse 38)? _____
_____

VERSE 19
Who causes us to not understand and accept the message about the kingdom (see verse 39)? _____

VERSE 20-21
Rocky ground represents hearers who _____ receive the Word, but when _____ comes, they _____

How can you apply this with company coming or a big ball game on Sunday?

VERSE 22
Thorny ground represents hearers who will not respond to God's Word because the _____ of this life _____
_____ choke it out.

How can you apply this to studying for a job promotion at work and studying for a big soul promotion in heaven?

DAY FOUR:

VERSE 23
The good soil represents those who _____ the word, _____ the word, and are blessed with reading, believing, and following more and more of God's word with joy.

VERSE 24-30

Coordinated With the Other Three Gospels

If the seed sown by Jesus is the Word of God, what do you think is the seed that produces weeds, and who does it originate with?
_____
_____

Do you think there are religious leaders today who sow beliefs that are not really part of the Bible? _____.

(See 1 Timothy 4:3 and Colossians 2:18, for example, that was predicted.)

VERSE 31-32
The kingdom of heaven is like a _____.
Though it is the _____ of seeds, it becomes a
_____

VERSE 33
How has the kingdom of heaven developed on earth like yeast?
_____
_____

VERSE 41
The weeds of mankind are those who cause _____
and do _____

VERSE 42
What do you think Jesus is describing as the destination of those who do evil? _____

Since all have sinned (see Romans 3:23), are we all condemned? _____ Read Revelation 21:8 that lists some sins that are called pure "evil". List them below. Are you surprised at any of them?
_____
_____
_____

_____
_____
_____
_____
_____

Matthew's Life of Christ

VERSE 43
Only when the evil ones are separated from those trying to follow the Father will they be able to _____ like the _____.

VERSE 47-50
What would happen to the good fish if the bad fish were not thrown away? _____ What do you think heaven would be like if those who refused to obey God were there? _____

VERSE 55
Did the people say Jesus WAS the son of the carpenter or IS the son of the carpenter? _____ Look at John 6:42. Did they say they KNEW Joseph or KNOW Joseph? _____

NOTE: Joseph was still alive the first year of Jesus' ministry, but apparently dead by the time of his crucifixion when Jesus asked John to take his mother, Mary, into his home. We have no evidence that Jesus performed a miracle to save Joseph's life.

Considering the glorious life in heaven, do you think he would have been doing Joseph a favor to keep him from heaven? _____

Who were Jesus' brothers? _____

VERSE 56
They also referred to his sisterS, indicating he had more than one or two.

DAY FIVE:

Matthew Chapter 14
John the Baptist Executed

VERSE 1

Coordinated With the Other Three Gospels

Who was the tetrarch (governor) at the time of Jesus? _____

NOTE: Herod was the family name. His father, Herod the Great, is the one who killed the babies in Bethlehem and who died while Jesus was being hidden in Egypt. Herod Antipas was the Tetrarch of Galilee. Herod Philip was the Tetrarch of all the provinces north and east of the Jordan River except Perea. Antipas and Philip were brothers.

VERSE 3-4
Whose wife had Herod Antipas married? _____
_____

NOTE: Josephus says Harold Antipas' first wife's father was the king of Arabia. He was so angry, he attacked the destroyed the palace. This happened around 4 BC, and now it was around 27 AD.

VERSE 6-8
The daughter of _____ danced at Herod's _____ party. Her mother told her to ask for the _____ of _____ as a reward for her dancing.

VERSE 9
Even though he did not want to, Herod agreed because he had given his _____. Do people today tend to honor their own word? _____

VERSE 13
Why did Jesus withdraw to a solitary place? _____
_____

VERSE 14-15
The crowd desperately followed Jesus as soon as they spotted him, without going home first to get some _____ to take along.

VERSE 17
In the entire hungry crowd, the apostles were able to find only
_____
_____
and _____

Matthew's Life of Christ

VERSE 20
How much of the bread and fish was left over? _____
_____

VERSE 21
How many families did Jesus feed? _____
_____

DAY SIX:

VERSE 22
Why do you think Jesus had to make his disciples get into the boat? (Hint: Look at verse 24.) _____
_____

VERSE 23
Why did Jesus go into the mountain alone? (Remember verse 13 above.) _____
_____

VERSE 25
If the first watch of the night started at 6:00 PM and each watch lasted three hours, what time was it now? _____

VERSE 24
After all this time, how far out into the Sea of Galilee were they (see John 6:19)? _____

VERSE 25
Jesus came to them _____ on the _____ (NOTE: Since he walked so far and no one could see him, do you think he was having fun riding the waves? Do you think the human side of Jesus liked to have fun?) _____

VERSE 30
When Peter took his eyes off Jesus and began noticing the wind, he was _____ and began to _____

VERSE 31-32

Coordinated With the Other Three Gospels

Even though Jesus told Peter, "You of little _____" how did his faith compare with the other men who stayed on the boat? _____

Matthew's Life of Christ

Week Five

Matthew Chapter 15
Jesus Escapes to a Foreign Country

DAY ONE:

VERSE 1
Even though Jesus was in the northern province of Galilee by the Sea of Galilee, religious leaders came to question him all the way from the southern province of Judea and the capitol city of

_____

VERSE 2
These religious leaders acted as though it was a sin to break the _____ of the religious elders. Do today's religious leaders sometimes call things sin that are not in the Bible?
_____

VERSE 3
Jesus answered their question with a question. "Why do you break the _____ or _____ for the sake of the _____?" Which is more important? The traditions of the church of the commands of God? _____
_____

VERSE 4-6
In Jesus' day, the religious leaders were telling people not to help support their _____ and _____ , but devote the money to God. By putting such traditions first, they were _____ the word of God.

VERSE 8
Such people honor God with their _____ but not their _____

VERSE 9
"They _____ me in _____ because they follow _____ taught by _____.
VERSE 14

Coordinated With the Other Three Gospels

Jesus said that these religious leaders were
_____ leaders of _____

VERSE 19
Notice theft, lying, and slander are in the same sin category as murder, adultery, and other sexual sins. Do we have a tendency to talk about little sins and big sins? _____

VERSE 21
A couple days after hearing John the Baptist was executed, Jesus _____ that place and withdrew to _____, cities in Lebanon where Herod did not have jurisdiction.

DAY TWO:

VERSE 25
In desperation, the woman knelt and begged, "_____
" _____
_____."

VERSE 28
Jesus had just been condemning the religious leaders of his own country, and here is a foreign woman to whom he says, "You have
_____
_____ "
_____."

VERSE 29-31
Back by the Sea of Galilee, Jesus did what? _____
_____
_____

VERSE 32
So desperate were people to be with Jesus, they stayed with him how long without eating? _____
_____

Do we demonstrate that much desire to be with Jesus today?
_____

VERSE 34

Matthew's Life of Christ

This time, Jesus' disciples collected _____ loaves and a few _____ _____ to feed everyone.

VERSE 35-37
How much was left after everyone ate? _____
_____

VERSE 38
How many families did Jesus feed this time?
_____

Matthew Chapter 16
Jesus Escapes to Another Foreign Country

VERSE 1
Even though Jesus had just fed perhaps 15,000 people miraculously, the stubborn religious leaders refused to acknowledge it and still demanded to see a _____ from the sky.

VERSE 4
Jesus repeated what he'd told them the last time they demanded a sign, the sign of Jonah. What was the sign to be (see chapter 12, verse 40)? _____
_____

DAY THREE:

VERSE 5-6
Then Jesus' own disciples seemed to tempt him by "forgetting" to take along _____ on their next trip across the lake. Jesus warned them not to be unduly influenced by the _____ who demanded a sign.

VERSE 12
Jesus used yeast as a sign of false teachings of the _____
_____

Coordinated With the Other Three Gospels

NOTE: 1 Corinthians 5:5 says our _____ nature is represented by yeast. Verse 8, it says yeast represents _____ and _____ This explains the significance of using unleavened bread in the Lord's Supper.

VERSE 13-15
Once again, having made the religious leaders angry, Jesus escapes to another region, Caesar-ea Philippi, where Philip Herod was governor. In this city, Philip had erected a Temple in honor of Caesar, who was considered a god. It is here that Jesus asks his twelve disciples, "Who do you _____
_____?"

VERSE 16
Simon Peter answered, "You are the _____, the _____ of the _____."

VERSE 17
Jesus had nicknamed Simon at the beginning of his ministry (see John 1:42). Peter, in Greek in which the N.T. was written, is "Petros," meaning stone. Jesus said he would build his church on a _____ (In Greek, this word is "Petra.")

1 Corinthians 10:4 says the rock is who? _____
_____. Therefore, Jesus was saying he would build the church on the fact that he is the _____ of God.

VERSE 19
To whom was Jesus talking when he said he would give them the keys so that whatever they bound on earth would be bound in heaven (see Matthew 18:1,18, and John 20:19,23)?

_____

NOTE: The original Greek of the New Testament says whatever they bind on earth has already been bound in heaven.

VERSE 21
Jesus began preparing them for the inevitable: that the next time he went to Jerusalem he would be _____ and on the _____ day be _____ back to
_____

Matthew's Life of Christ

VERSE 22
Who objected? _____

VERSE 23
Jesus shouted back, "Get _____ me, _____!" You are a _____ _____ to me!"

Jesus was tempted in every way (Hebrews 4:15). Further, according to Hebrews 5:7 Jesus begged God with _____ cries and _____ to not have to be put to _____.

DAY FOUR:

VERSE 27
We will be rewarded by what each of us has _____ during our life, not prayers after we die.

VERSE 28
Jesus said some _____ there with him would not _____ before the kingdom/church came.

Matthew Chapter 17
Jesus' Body Transfigured/Transformed

VERSE 2
Jesus' figure was translated so that his face shone like the _____ and his clothes became as white as _____.

VERSE 3
Who appeared and began talking with Jesus? _____ _____ and _____.

Moses had died 2500 years earlier, and Elijah had died 900 years earlier. But they maintained their identity even in eternity. Luke 9:31 says they were talking about his _____ from this life. Do you think Jesus' human nature needed their eencouragement? _____

Coordinated With the Other Three Gospels

VERSE 4
Peter suggested they honor all three. Moses represented the Law of Moses in the Old Testament. Elijah represented all the prophets in the Old Testament trying to get people to obey the Law of Moses.

VERSE 5
A voice from heaven announced "This _____ is _____ , whom I _____ Listen to _____!"

From now on, the Law of Moses and the prophets of the Old Testament would be supplanted by Jesus. See Colossians 2:12-14.

VERSE 11-13
The three were quoting from the last book of the Old Testament, Malachi 4:5, predicting Elijah would announce the Savior's coming. Who did Jesus say was their modern-day Elijah? _____
_____

VERSE 14-16
When they rejoined the other nine disciples, it was learned that they could not heal a demon-possessed boy. Why couldn't they (see Mark 9:29)? _____
_____

VERSE 19-20
To whom did Jesus say nothing would be impossible? _____
_____

DAY FIVE:
VERSE 22-23
Once more Jesus tried to prepare his twelve disciples by telling them he would be _____ into the hands of men who would _____, but on the third day he would be _____

Do you think these men believed the last part of Jesus' prediction yet? _____

A LOT OF PEOPLE CALL THE APOSTLE THOMAS "DOUBTING THOMAS," BUT WHEN THE WOMEN WENT TO TELL THEM JESUS WAS ALIVE, NOT A SINGLE APOSTLE BELIEVED THEM.

Matthew's Life of Christ

VERSE 24
Rather than free-will offerings, a Temple tax was levied to support the headquarters of the Jewish religion. Their tax collectors traveled throughout the country collecting it.

VERSE 25-26
Taking another opportunity to teach a spiritual lesson, Jesus inferred that his followers would also be sons of God. Galatians 3:26-27 says we are all _____ of God if we were _____ into Christ.

Matthew Chapter 18
How We Should Try to Get Along

VERSE 1
Jesus' disciples asked Jesus "Who is the _____ _____ in the kingdom/church?".

VERSE 2-4
From this passage, do you think Jesus believed little children were sinners? _____

VERSE 6
If an adult causes a child to "sin," who is responsible for that sin?
_____

VERSE 7-9
Galatians 5:19-21 lists some sins. Are there any activities in our lives today that we should get out of (relationships, clubs, organizations, etc.) so we can get rid of our sinful acts or attitudes? Write down one. _____

VERSE 10
Do children have guardian angels?_____ _____
Do Christians (see Hebrews 1:14)? _____

VERSE 12-14
When a child of God falls away, what does God do? _____
_____

Coordinated With the Other Three Gospels

In what ways do you think God gets our attention today?
_____

DAY SIX:

VERSE 15
If someone offends us, should we gossip about them? _____
If not, what should we do? _____

VERSE 16
If we cannot settle it, we should return with two or three _____
_____

VERSE 17
If that does not work, we are to tell the whole church. If that does not work, we are to quit trying to restore them.

VERSE 20
How many worshiping or doing a good work together in Jesus' name does it take for Jesus to be there among them? _____

VERSE 21-22
How many times are we to forgive someone who sins against us?
_____

VERSE 23-24
A man in Jesus' parable owed someone _____ talents of gold bouillon that he could not repay.

VERSE 27
But the holder of the IOU decided to completely _____ the debt.

VERSE 28-30
Yet, the debtor turned right around the had arrested a man owing him _____ denarii (under $100) and sent him to
_____

VERSE 31-34
So the holder of the first IOU for millions took this man and had him tortured.

Matthew's Life of Christ

Week Six

Matthew Chapter 19
AD 30 ~ Jesus Talks About Family

DAY ONE:

VERSE 1
Jesus now left _____ for the very last time and headed toward the province of _____ at the other end of the country where Jerusalem was located.

VERSE 2-3
Among the large crowds that followed him were the hypocritical religious leaders. They gave him another entrapment question, one that is not popular even today. What was it? _____
_____

VERSE 4-6
Jesus quoted the first book of the Bible, Genesis 2:24 where God created Adam and Eve, and said the two would become _____ flesh. Then Jesus said what is often repeated at weddings: "What _____ has _____ together, let _____ not _____ ."

VERSE 7
Trying to show that the Bible contradicts itself, they reminded Jesus that Moses allowed a man to give his wife a _____ of _____

VERSE 8
Jesus replied that God conceded to let them because of the _____ of their hearts.

NOTE: God had conceded on other things because of the hardness of their heart. He told them not to have a king because he was their king, but later relented, though warning them their kings would be their downfall.

VERSE 9

Coordinated With the Other Three Gospels

Jesus then said they should return to the way marriage was set up in the beginning and only divorce for marital _____

VERSE 13-15
Here's Jesus around children again! His apostles thought Jesus was too dignified for children. But Jesus set, "Let the _____ come to me...for the kingdom of heaven belongs to such as _____

VERSE 17
Jesus said to enter eternal life, we must do more than just believe he was the Son of God. We also have to _____ _____ the _____.

DAY TWO:

VERSE 18f
Jesus then repeated six of the Ten Commandments of Moses, which involved the treatment of people toward other people. They are _____
_____
_____
_____
_____

VERSE 21
Jesus was not against people having wealth. Luke 8:2-3 says wealthy women helped support him while he traveled. Also, Matthew 27:57 says a rich man named Joseph had become a ___ _____. Why do you think he told this young man to get rid of all his wealth? _____
_____
_____

VERSE 22
Was Jesus just trying to give this young man a hard time? Look at Mark 10:21. How did Jesus feel about him? _____
_____ How do we tend to treat people we love? _____
_____

Matthew's Life of Christ

VERSE 23
Jesus said it was _____ (but not impossible) for the _____ to enter the _____ Of God.

VERSE 24
Jesus said it was easier for a _____ to go through the _____ of a _____ than for a _____ man to enter he kingdom of God.

VERSE 25
Knowing everyone wants riches, his disciples said that made it impossible for anyone to be _____.

VERSES 26
Even though this is impossible, Jesus reassured them it is not impossible with _____.

VERSE 29f
In what way can we have more brothers and sisters than ever in the church in this life? _____

_____

What other reward will we receive? _____

DAY THREE:

Matthew Chapter 20
Jesus' New Kingdom, the Church

VERSE 1
The kingdom/church is like men being hired _____ in the morning to work all _____ for a certain salary.

VERSE 3-6
Men were also hired at the _____ hour, the _____ hour, the _____ hour, and the _____ hour, all for the same pay.

VERSE 11-12

Coordinated With the Other Three Gospels

Those who had worked all day for their agreed-on pay were angry because those hired to work only _____ hour were paid the _____.

VERSE 13-16
How does this make the person feel who becomes a Christian late in life? _____ In God's eyes, was it a wasted life? _____

VERSE 17-19
Once more Jesus took his twelve apostles aside to warn them he was going to be condemned to _____, then _____ and _____ and finally _____. But three days later he was going to be _____ back to _____.

VERSE 20
Zebedee's sons were James and John (remember Matthew 3:21?) and were among the first of the twelve apostles selected. Their mother asked Jesus if they could be second and third in Jesus' coming _____

Do you think she thought he was getting ready to set up a physical kingdom on earth as soon as he got to Jerusalem?

VERSE 21-22
Jesus was upset because he knew, to be great in the kingdom, one had to give the most. When he asked them, "Can you drink the _____ I am going to drink, he was using an old Jewish custom of speaking of very bad times as drinking from a cup of wrath.

VERSE 23
Who will be allowed to sit with Jesus on his throne (see Revelation 3:21)? _____

DAY FOUR:

VERSE 25-28
What does it take to be great in the kingdom/church? _____
_____

Matthew's Life of Christ

VERSE 29
Now Jesus is in Jericho, a city near Jerusalem. Two _____ _____ men called him _____ and the _____ of David. Notice the word Son is in capitals. They were recognizing him as the long-promised Savior.

VERSE 32-34
Even though Jesus was headed doggedly toward his own torture and martyrdom, he took time to do what? _____

Matthew Chapter 21
Triumphant Entry Into Jerusalem

VERSE 2
Jesus sent two of his disciples to Bethphage to find a _____ and her _____.

VERSE 3
He was so well known by this time, all the disciples had to do to explain why they were taking these animals was to say, "The _____ needs them."

VERSE 5
This fulfilled the prophecy made five centuries earlier that he would arrive in Zion (Jerusalem) lowly because he was riding on the donkey's colt ~ the baby, not the grow mother.

NOTE: Riding a donkey was not lowly. Riding a donkey was a sign of royalty. All Jewish kings rode donkeys then. In the Old Testament, a certain supreme judge over Israel had 30 sons who ruled 30 cities, and each had a donkey to ride (Judges 10:30). About 1000 BC, the time of David, royalty began riding mules. All King David's sons rode mules (2 Samuel 13:29). When David made his son king, he had Solomon ride his own personal mule as proof (1 Kings 1:33, 38, 44).

VERSE 7

Coordinated With the Other Three Gospels

Jesus had the donkey beside him (the executive limousine) while he rode the colt (golf art). That is what made him a gentle king. He did not even have a saddle; his apostles spread their _____ on the colt.

VERSE 8
As he neared Jerusalem, large crowds of people spread out the "red carpet" for him, placing their own _____ on the road for the donkey to walk on.

They also cut _____ and spread those on the road for the donkey to walk on.

NOTE: This was a custom the Jews normally observed during the Feast of Harvest kept every October celebrating their original entry into the Promised Land 2500 years earlier, and also the Day of Atonement. The Jews believed Jesus was going to take over their country and return it to them, getting rid of the foreign occupation government sent there by Caesar.

Leviticus 23:39 (part of the Law of Moses directed toward the Levite tribe), explains, "On the first day you are to take choice fruit from the trees, and palm fronds, leafy branches and poplars, and rejoice before the Lord your God for seven days."

DAY FIVE:

VERSE 9
Then crowds began shouting _____ (meaning Savior) to the _____ of David!"

NOTE: They were quoting from Psalm 118, which people normally sang at the Feast of Harvest. Notice especially verses 22-27:

> *The stone the builders rejected has become the capstone;*
> *The Lord has done this, and it is marvelous in our eyes.*
> *This is the day the Lord has made;*
> *Let us rejoice and be glad in it.*
> *O Lord, save us! O Lord, grant us success.*
> *BLESSED IS HE WHO COMES IN THE NAME OF THE LORD.*
> *From the house of the Lord we bless you.*
> *The Lord is God, and he has made his light shine upon us.*

Matthew's Life of Christ

WITH BOUGHS IN HAND
JOIN IN THE FESTAL PROCESSION
Up to the horns of the altar.

VERSE 10
How much of the city of Jerusalem was stirred by the parade?
_____

NOTE: Josephus said there were normally nearly three million people there during the Feast of Passover.

VERSE 12
Jesus went to the _____ area (courtyard) where they were buying and selling things. (The entire temple complex was the size of several football fields.) He overturned the tables of the _____
_____ (who turned foreign currency into temple currency, charging a hefty fee which they pocketed), and the benches of those _____
(making a profit from their sacrifices, rather than let them buy off the street).

VERSE 13
If we go overboard in buying and selling in our church buildings, can they reach a point of no longer being a house of prayer?
_____

VERSE 14
Jesus is now just a few days away from his betrayal, torture, and execution, but he still takes time to do what? _____
_____

VERSE 15
Were the priests and teachers of the religious law happy (see Luke 19:47-48)? _____ Why (see John 12:19)?
_____

VERSE 19-20
Did Jesus punish the fig tree for not having fruit on it for their breakfast, or did he merely take advantage of another seemingly insignificant event to teach a lesson (see also John 15:12)?
_____

56

Coordinated With the Other Three Gospels

VERSE 21-22
Since neither Jesus nor anyone else ever willed a mountain into the sea, do you think Jesus was promising help from God for material things or spiritual things? Hint: Look at Hebrews 12:22-24a.

DAY SIX:

VERSE 23
No longer is it local religious leaders, but the religious hierarchy that now approaches Jesus. The _____ priests and _____ iindignantly demanded to know by what _____ he turned those tables over out in the temple lobby.

VERSE 24-27
Jesus answered their question with a question of his own. Did they reply that baptism wasn't necessary in order to get out of answering him? _____ Did they answer his question at all? _____ Why? _____ Why do you think Jesus did not enter into a debate with them? _____

VERSE 28-31
Then Jesus asked them a question in parable form. One son agreed to work, but did _____. The other so said he wouldn't, but then _____. Ultimately, which one was obedient? _____ _____ Jesus inferred that they, who claimed to do what God the Father told them to were not doing it; but tax _____ and _____ _____ were the ones who followed John's teachings. The religious leaders believed they had nothing to repent of.

VERSE 33-39
Now that Jesus had the attention of the religious hierarchy, and he has taught his followers all they need to know, he is prepared to force their hand into showing openly how much they hate true LOVE.

Matthew's Life of Christ

In this parable, a _____ left
some farmers in charge of his vineyard. But whenever he sent
someone to collect the harvest, what did they do to him?
_____

Finally, they even killed his _____.
Who do you think Jesus was referring to when he told about the
son?

VERSE 42
Jesus then quotes from a verse in a Psalm that the crowd probably
shouted on his Triumphal Entry into Jerusalem: "The
_____ the builders
_____ has become the
_____

VERSE 43-44
Then Jesus boldly told them outright: "The kingdom of
_____ will be _____
_____

VERSE 45-46
So, the chief priests and Pharisees looked harder for a way to
_____ Jesus.

Coordinated With the Other Three Gospels

Week Seven

Matthew Chapter 22
Jesus' Showdown With Religious Hierarchy

DAY ONE

VERSE 1-2
Still pushing them to show their true colors, Jesus told them the kingdom of heaven is like a wedding banquet for God's _____. Remember from Ephesians 5:25-32 who the wife of Christ is? _____

VERSE 3
The first ones God invited _____ to come.

(The Jews were the first ones invited. Later the Gentiles would be invited.)

VERSE 4
So the father of the groom sent people to beg them to come to the _____ banquet, the marriage of his son to the church.

VERSE 7
Would God be a good God to allow people to destroy the chances of everyone else to become part of his church? _____

VERSE 10
What kind of people came to the wedding? _____ _____ and _____

VERSE 11-12
God was angry when someone tried to come to the wedding of the church to Jesus without _____
_____

Matthew's Life of Christ

NOTE: In those days, wedding clothes were offered at the door to everyone. Only someone refusing them and sneaking in would not be wearing them. What do the wedding clothes represent (see Revelation 1:5-6; and 7:14,)? _____
_____
_____
_____
_____

VERSE 13
So why would the person who sneaked into the church be thrown out? _____

VERSE 14
How many does God invite to be at the church's wedding? _____ How many accept? _____

VERSE 20-21
Jesus asked for a coin when challenged whether they should pay taxes to the foreign occupation government. (If he said yes, he'd make the Jews mad; if he said no, he'd make Rome mad.) He then asked whose portrait and name were on it. They replied _____. So he said, "Give to _____ what is _____ And to _____ what is _____.

DAY TWO:

VERSE 23:
The Sadducee religious sect believed there is no _____ _____, so tried their own entrapment question.

VERSE 24-28
They asked him that, if a woman married _____ times, who would she be married to in heaven.

VERSE 29
Jesus answered that in heaven people will not _____, but be as the _____.

VERSE 31-32
Then he went on to correct their false belief that we are not

Coordinated With the Other Three Gospels

resurrected after we die. He cited in the Old Testament that God said, "_____ the God of _____." God is not the God of the _____ but the _____

VERSE 34-38
Now it is the Pharisees' turn again. So they asked him to show favoritism for one of the Laws of Moses. He did not mention any of the Ten Commandments. Instead, he said, "_____ _____ the Lord your God with all your _____, all your _____, and all your _____."

VERSE 39
He said the second greatest commandment is "_____ your _____ as _____."

VERSE 40
Every one of the approximately 600 laws in the Old Testament are summed up in these _____ commandments.

VERSE 41-44
Jesus now matches the intelligence of the religious scholars by putting a theological question to them: According to many prophecies, the Christ was to be the son of _____. Yet, David in one of his psalms said, "_____ Lord said to _____ Lord, sit at my _____ _____."

VERSE 45
Then he asks them how he can be David's son and his Lord at the same time. They knew he was a descendant of David. But they did not want to admit he was also the Son of _____.

DAY THREE:

Matthew Chapter 23
Jesus Condemns Hypocrite Religious Leaders

VERSE 1-3

Matthew's Life of Christ

Jesus then told the crowd they had to obey what the religious leaders say, but warned them not to _____ what they _____ because the do not _____ _____ what they _____.

VERSE 4
The religious hierarchy was putting heavy loads of minute rules and regulations which they themselves were not willing to _____ a _____ _____ to help with.

VERSE 5
Everything the religious hierarchy was doing was for men to _____. That included tying little boxes (phylacteries) on their foreheads containing scriptures.

VERSE 6
They loved the places of _____ and the most important _____.

VERSE 7
They insisted on being called by the title _____

Thought Question: Do religious leaders today insist on being called a title? _____

VERSE 8
Jesus told the people not to give religious titles to religious leaders because ultimately they all have one Savior and are all _____.

VERSE 9
He also told them not to call anyone on earth _____ in a religious sense, for we have only _____ Father, and he is in _____.

VERSE 10
Nor were they to call anyone by the title _____ _____ in a religious sense, because their only true Teacher is _____.

VERSE 12

Coordinated With the Other Three Gospels

If we _____ ourselves, we will ultimately be _____. If we _____ ourselves, we will ultimately be _____.

DAY FOUR:

VERSE 13-14
Jesus accused the religious hierarchy of shutting the _____ _____ of _____ in people's _____. They did not want to do what was necessary to enter the church, and did not want anyone else to either.

Jesus is getting really mad. Their petty rules were destroying people.

VERSE 15
Even though they were religious teachers, he said they were _____ of hell. Pretty strong language. It was his last effort to get them to acknowledge it and ask for forgiveness and change their ways. Some did, but not many. Name one who did (see John 3:1 & 5): _____ _____

VERSE 23
They insisted that people tithe even the smallest seeds. Yet they neglected _____, _____ _____ and _____

VERSE 25
With strong language, Jesus declared they insisted on clean dishes, but inside they were full of _____ and _____

VERSE 27-28
Jesus is probably shouting at them by now. He said the religious hierarchy was like _____
_____
They were beautiful on the outside, but inside were _____
_____
In other words, they appeared to be _____ _____, but inside they were just

Matthew's Life of Christ

VERSE 29-32
Jesus said they decorated the tombs of the _____,
and claimed they wouldn't have killed them had they lived then, but they are just like them. (He knew they were about to kill him, too.)

Can you see the veins in his neck pulsate as he makes his final judgment?

VERSE 33
Then Jesus told them outright that they were all going to _____

VERSE 37-39
Now Jesus turns and walks away, possibly with tears. As he left the temple (which is on the highest point of Jerusalem), he said to the city that he'd longed to _____
_____ as a _____
_____
but they refused.

DAY FIVE

Matthew Chapter 24
Jesus Predicts the Beginning of the Church

NOTE: Many people believe Jesus was talking about the destruction of the temple and end of the world.

VERSE 1-2
As he was leaving, Jesus' twelve disciples commented on the huge Temple. Jesus predicted that not one _____ would be left on another.

Psalm 118:22 in the Old Testament predicted that Jesus would the chief cornerstone that the builders would reject. So, when they crucified him, the whole system of Judaism collapsed with him.

Coordinated With the Other Three Gospels

In John 2:19-22, Jesus considered his body the temple and said that, when the Jewish leaders destroyed it, he would raise it up in three days.

VERSE 3
Jesus' apostles asked them the following questions:

(1) _____will this destruction of the "temple" happen?
(2) What will be the _____ of Jesus coming and the _____ of the _____,

VERSE 4-6
"Let no one _____ you. Many will claim to be the Messiah (anointed king), there will be wars, but that will _____ be the sign of the end.

VERSE 7
There will be famines and earthquakes.

Amos 8:11 predicted a spiritual famine of not hearing and heeding the words of _____.

VERSE 8
But that will only be the _____(not the end!) -- the birth _____.

VERSE 9
This is how the religious leaders of the day treated Jesus' apostles while he was still with them.

Matthew 14:6-12 told us how John the Baptist was jailed and beheaded during Jesus' time of preaching.

VERSE 10
Later in Matthew 26:20-25, it will tell about Jesus' betrayal.

DAY SIX:

VERSES 11-28
Many details of the tribulation the Jewish priests put Jesus and his apostles through are given, as well as others trying to take power away from Rome so they could rule their own country.

Matthew's Life of Christ

VERSE 29
Then the sun will become _____.

Later in Matthew 27:45, it says there was darkness for three hours while Jesus was on the cross.

Also, the _____ of heavenly places (spirit world) will be _____.

Jesus said days before his crucifixion in John 12:31 and 32, "Now the prince of this world will be driven out" and, when he is crucified, he will draw all men to him and away from Satan. Ephesians 2:2 calls Satan the prince of the powers of the air.

VERSE 30
Now Jesus discusses their second question regarding the sign of the end of the age.

Remember, when the Bible called Jesus the cornerstone? When they killed him, the Jewish age collapsed and then a new age began – the Christ-ian age. (Hebrews 10:1 & 9-11 explains this.)

So, the end of the Christian age will come when Jesus appears in the _____.

First, everyone throughout the world will _____
Jesus coming on the _____.

VERSE 31
Second, Jesus will send his _____
with a loud _____ call, and they will gather
his _____. Who are God's elect (see 2
Timothy 2:8-11)? _____
How does one die with him (Rom. 6:4)? _____
_____

VERSE 34
Finally, Jesus gets specific when the things will happen before the en. "This _____ will not die before _____ will happen. FINAL ANSWER TO THEIR QUESTION 1.

Coordinated With the Other Three Gospels

(IN HIS APOSTLES' GENERATON, NOT THOUSANDS OF YEARS LATER.)

VERSE 36
THEN HE ANSWERS QUESTION 2.

how many people know the date when Jesus will return in the sky on the Day of Judgment? _____

VERSE 44
Jesus will return at an hour when we _____
_____

VERSE 47-51
Everyone, even the servant that beats his fellow servants, will be assigned a place with the _____ where there is _____ and _____ of teeth.

Matthew's Life of Christ

Week Eight

Matthew Chapter 25
Parables & Parallels

DAY ONE:

VERSE 1
In this parable explaining the end of the world, Jesus said there were _____ virgins (bridesmaid friends of the bride and groom) waiting for the _____ to arrive so they could escort him into the bride's home.

VERSE 6-8
When it was announced at _____ that the bridegroom was on his way, the foolish ones tried to get the wise virgins to give them some of their _____

They were also foolish enough to think a shop would be open at midnight!

VERSE 9-10
So, while they were gone, the _____
_____ arrived and they escorted him to the _____
_____. (They couldn't make the bridegroom wait for his own wedding!)

VERSE 11-13
Once the door was closed, they could not let anyone else in (it was the middle of the night and too dangerous.) So when the foolish virgins called out for them to open the door, the door guard said, "I don't _____. It will be the same way when Jesus comes. Then it will be too late.

What does the lamp represent in Jesus' parable? Remember Mathew 5:14-16. _____
_____

VERSE 19-23
When the master returned and saw the results of the first

Coordinated With the Other Three Gospels

man's work, he put him in charge of _____
_____. When he saw the result of the
second man's work, he put him in charge of_____
_____

VERSE 24-27
The one who buried his talent came to the conclusion that the
master was a _____ man so wouldn't take
any chances of working with what he got. The master replied that if
that was the way he felt, he should have at least put it on _____
_____ with the bankers for _____.

VERSE 28-30
Then the one who refused to work, using as his excuse that he had
a hard master, was thrown _____ into the
_____
where there is _____ and
gnashing _____.

VERSE 34-39
He will reward people who used their talents in the following ways: "I
was _____ _____ and you gave me something to
_____. I was _____ and you
gave me something to _____. I was a
_____ and you
_____ me in."

VERSE 41-46
But those who did not help anyone he will send to _____.

DAY TWO

Matthew Chapter 26
Jesus Introduces the Lord's Supper, then Agonizes Over His Death

VERSE 3-4
The _____
And _____
Assembled in the palace of the_____
_____ and _____

Matthew's Life of Christ

how to arrest Jesus and _____ him.

VERSE 6
While Jesus was eating at a home in Bethany near Jerusalem, a woman poured very _____ on his head.

NOTE: In those days, Jews anointed a man to be king or high priest. Perhaps, since Jesus did not take over as high priest and king during his Triumphant Entry, she decided to anoint him herself to show he was her high priest and her king.

(Toward the end of the Old Testament in Zechariah, God told the people through a prophet that they should combine the office of high priest and king through one man.)

VERSE 12
Jesus gave a different significance to this anointing, however. He announced she had done it to _____ him for his _____ (they embalmed with spices.)

VERSE 14-15
_____ went to the _____ and agreed to hand Jesus over to them for how much money? _____
_____

NOTE: In Bible times, one piece of silver was worth about 11-1/2 days' wages, so 30 pieces would be worth about 1-1/2 years' pay. Also, in Bible times, it cost 30 pieces of silver to purchase a slave.

VERSE 17
Verse one says they were about to keep the Passover. In this verse, it is called what? _____
_____.

VERSE 21
As soon as they began eating, Jesus announced, "_____ of you will _____ me." In so doing, he gave Judas a chance to back out.

Coordinated With the Other Three Gospels

NOTE: The other three biographies of Jesus say Judas left the table at this point and went out to make arrangements to betray Jesus later that night. So he was not part of the new religious ceremony Jesus established ~ the Lord's Supper.

VERSE 26

NOTE: The Passover began about 2500 BC when Moses led the Israelites out of Egypt and slavery. On their last night before being released, God passed over Egypt. Any family that had the blood of a lamb on their doorpost was safe, so God PASSED OVER them. But any family that refused to put the blood of a lamb on their doorpost suffered the loss of their firstborn son.

So every year on this date, the Jews kept the Passover Feast, which included a lamb that was eaten, unleavened bread (they were in a hurry to leave), wine, and bitter herbs (reminding them of the bitterness of their slavery).

So now, when Jesus passed around the unleavened bread to be eaten, he gave it a new meaning. He said that now this unleavened bread represented what? _____

NOTE: It was not literally his body, for he was still in his body and talking to them. 1 Peter 1:19 says we were redeemed (bought from slavery to sin) with the precious _____ of _____ a _____ without blemish.

VERSE 27-28
The fruit of the vine (wine/grape juice) represented freedom. Jesus said, "This is _____ of the new covenant."

NOTE: "Covenant" is also translated "testament". He was setting up a new system of worship. No longer would people worship with the ceremonies given in the Law of Moses in the Old Testament/Covenant.

VERSE 29
Jesus said he would partake of this again when the kingdom came. When did he partake of it next (Acts 10:41)? _____
_____

Matthew's Life of Christ

VERSE 30
What kind of music did they have as part of this ceremony? Vocal, instrumental, or both? _____ Although he was establishing a new ceremony, he did not have an evening of singing with choirs, organs, orchestra, or anything fancy. They sang just one hymn, then left.

DAY THREE:

VERSE 32-35
Peter and the other disciples announced they would never fall away. But Jesus said that very _____ Peter would _____ him _____ times.

VERSE 38
Jesus became very troubled. He said his soul was _____ _____ _____.

NOTE: Since crucifixion was a common form of execution by the Romans in that day, do you think there was anything else bothering him (see 2 Corinthians 5:19 and 21)? _____ _____.

VERSE 39
Even at the last minute, the Son was begging the Father/Will, "May this _____ (of suffering) be _____ _____."

VERSE 40
Then he returned to his apostles, probably for some encouragement, and found them _____.
He told them, "The spirit is _____, but the _____."

VERSE 47
Judas arrived with a large _____
Armed with _____
and _____ sent from the _____
_____

Coordinated With the Other Three Gospels

and _____.

NOTE: John 18:3 says it was a cohort of Roman soldiers – a battalion of 600+ men. Do you think Judas warned them how powerful Jesus was? _____

VERSE 48-49
Since there were no newspapers or TV then, even well-known people often were not recognized. So what kind of signal did Judas give to indicate which one was Jesus?_____
_____

VERSE 51
One of Jesus' disciples (John 18:10 says it was Peter) did what?
_____
_____.

Luke 22:51 says Jesus replaced the man's ear.

VERSE 53
Jesus, knowing his time had come, said he could call more than _____ of _____ to defend him.

NOTE: Twelve legions would be the size of an entire army. At that time, Rome's army numbered nearly half a million.

VERSE 56
Jesus told the soldiers to leave them alone. Then what did his disciples do?_____

VERSE 58
Although we condemn Peter for betraying Jesus, at least he followed him right up to the _____ of the _____

DAY FOUR:

VERSE 59
The religious hierarchy looked for _____
_____
against Jesus.

Matthew's Life of Christ

VERSE 61
They finally got him on a charge of destruction of religious property because he said he would destroy the _____
But it was not enough for a death sentence.

VERSE 65-66
Thus far, they bungled his execution, so with Jesus' own help (he said he was God), they finally got enough evidence to announce he was worthy of _____.

VERSE 67
How did the religious hierarchy treat him? _____
_____
_____

VERSE 75
When the rooster crowed as predicted by Jesus, what did Peter do?
_____
_____

Matthew Chapter 27
The Crucifixion

VERSE 1-2
The chief priests and elders handed Jesus over to _____
_____ , the _____
because only the Romans were allowed to put someone to death at this time.

VERSE 3
What surprised Judas? _____

Jesus could command storms. What do you think Judas thought Jesus would do that he did not do?
_____
_____

VERSE 4-5

Coordinated With the Other Three Gospels

Judas confessed, "I have _____." He even threw the _____ at the priests and elders in remorse. At this point, he had the same remorse Peter had when he betrayed Jesus. What did Judas then do that Peter did not? _____
_____

NOTE: Later, Peter would write this (see 1 Peter 2:1-2): "Therefore, rid yourselves of all malice and all deceit, hypocrisy, envy, and slander of every kind. Like newborn babies crave pure spiritual milk, so that by it you may grow up in your salvation." Peter knew how to learn from his mistakes and START ALL OVER.

VERSE 7
What did the priests and elders do with the money? _____
_____

VERSE 9-10
Without realizing it, they fulfilled yet another prophecy involving Jesus which was spoken by _____ seven centuries earlier.

DAY FIVE:

VERSE 11-13
When Governor Pilate questioned Jesus personally, Jesus answered. But when the priests and elders arrived to accuse him, Jesus refused to answer. Do you have any idea why? (Verse 18 & 23f might help.) _____
_____
_____

VERSE 17
Who was Bar Abbas? _____
_____
_____

VERSE 19
How did Pilate's wife feel about Jesus? _____
_____
_____

Matthew's Life of Christ

VERSE 20-23
When given a chance to have one political prisoner sentenced to death to be freed, the crowd chose to free who? _____
_____
What did they insist Pilate do to Jesus? _____
_____

VERSE 24
What did Pilate do and say the crowd? _____
_____
_____

VERSE 26
Then Pilate had Jesus _____.

NOTE: What they did was strip him to his waist and beat him with a whip that had rough chunks of iron tied on it every foot or so. Many men died of it.

VERSE 27-29
In Jesus' weakened condition, what did the soldiers do to him next?
_____
_____
_____
What did they say to him? _____
_____
_____

VERSE 30
What did they do to him after that? _____
_____
_____

NOTE: By the time they took the robe off him, his blood would have clotted and then the wounds re-opened.

VERSE 31
According to Mark 15:22, they brought him to Golgotha ("Skull Hill"). The word "brought" in the original Greek manuscripts means they carried him. Jesus was so weak by this time, the soldiers had to literally carry him up the hill to finish killing him.

Coordinated With the Other Three Gospels

VERSE 32
On their way, they forced a man named _____
to _____ Jesus' _____.

DAY SIX:

VERSE 34
Why do you think Jesus refused the painkillers?
_____
_____

VERSE 37
What did the sign designating his crime say? _____
_____
_____

VERSE 38
What other criminals were crucified at the same time? _____
_____
_____

VERSE 40
What did the taunts of the crowds have in common with Satan's taunts three years earlier when he tempted Jesus in the wilderness (see Matthew 4:3 and 6)? What is the phrase they all repeated?
_____

VERSE 42
Do you think the chief priests, theology teachers, and elders really would have believed Jesus had he come down from the cross? _____ Why? _____
_____
_____

VERSE 44
Who else insulted Jesus? _____
_____

VERSE 45
Jesus was crucified the third hour of the day (see Mark 15:25), which would be 9:00. Beginning at _____ o'clock, to _____ o'clock, there was _____

Matthew's Life of Christ

_____

VERSE 46
At 3:00 he cried loudly, "_____
why have you _____?"

NOTE: God only forsakes those who have sinned against him. In the Old Testament 700 years before Jesus, Isaiah said, "Yet, it was OUR grief he bore, OUR sorrows that weighed him down. And we thought his problems were a punishment from God for his OWN sins.

VERSE 48
Jesus finally accepted a small drink of _____
from a sponge.

NOTE: The *Merck Manual of Diagnosis and Therapy* says anyone in severe shock (obviously, this was one of the things Jesus was suffering from) should never be given liquids by mouth, "as it often results in sudden death." Apparently, Jesus was now ready to die and knew what to do to bring it about.

John 19:30 says that, after his drink, he said, "It is _____
_____." He had fulfilled the Law of Moses by keeping all 600+ commandments his entire life in a human body. He was perfect and sinless.

VERSE 50
When Jesus had _____ out again in a _____
voice, he _____
his _____.

VERSE 51
Immediately the _____ shook and the
_____ split (earthquake), and at that
moment the _____ of the _____
_____ was _____
in two from _____ to _____.

NOTE: This curtain was the room divider hiding the Most Holy Place in the Temple. Only one person was ever allowed to enter it ~ the high priest ~ and even then only once a year on the Day of Atonement (see Hebrews 9:1-7).

Coordinated With the Other Three Gospels

Jesus became our high priest and entered the spiritual Most Holy Place in heaven (Hebrews 9:8-1). With the curtain torn, Jesus began the New Last Will and Testament of God (Hebrews 9:15-16).

VERSE 52-53
Also at that moment the _____
Broke _____ and the _____
of many holy people who had _____
were _____
_____
They stayed near their graves until after Jesus' _____
_____ at which time they entered Jerusalem.

VERSE 54
What did the centurion exclaim upon seeing all this? _____
_____
_____

VERSE 57-60
Rich Joseph took Jesus' mangled and bloody body off the cross, getting Jesus' blood all over his clothes, and placed it in his own
_____
Then he rolled a _____ in front of the entrance.

VERSE 66
The chief priests wanted to make sure no one stole Jesus' body to fool people into believing he came back to life, so Pilate gave them permission to _____ it by putting a (concrete) _____ on the stone and posting _____
_____

Matthew Chapter 28
Jesus' Resurrection and Great Commission

VERSE 1
Why did the Christians begin worshipping on the first day of the week (Sunday), instead of the seventh day of the week (Saturday)? HINT: Look at verse 6. _____

Matthew's Life of Christ

VERSE 2

Who rolled away the stone? _____

NOTE: The Greek that the New Testament was written in indicates the stone flew out of its track.

VERSE 4
The guards saw it, but became so _____
_____, they _____ and became like _____ men.

VERSE 5-9
Who were the first to see Jesus after he returned to life?
_____
_____
_____

VERSE 11-13
When the guards reported what had happened, the religious hierarchy bribed the soldiers to say Jesus' _____
_____ came during the _____
and _____ him away.

VERSE 19
What was the first half of Jesus' great commission to them?
_____ and make _____
of all nations, _____
them in the name of the _____.
The _____,
and the _____.

Romans 6:3-4 says that, in baptism, we have the privilege of imitating what Jesus did for us. Write these 2 verses out here:
_____
_____
_____
_____
_____
_____

Coordinated With the Other Three Gospels

VERSE 20
What is the second half of Jesus' great commission to them?
_____ them to _____
_____ everything I have _____
_____ you.

NOTE: This shows that baptism is necessary, but it alone cannot save us. It also shows that obeying Jesus' other commands alone will not save us either. What does it show? _____
_____
_____

If we do these things, Jesus promised to be with us how long?
_____

A Few of Many Predictions Jesus Fulfilled in His Lifetime

Born of a virgin (Isaiah 7:14 and Matthew 1:23)
Born in Bethlehem (Micah 5:2 and Matthew 2:6)
Babies killed after birth (Jeremiah 31:15 and Matthew 2:16-18)
Escaped to Egypt (Hosea 11:1 and Matthew 2:15)
Exact year he'd begin teaching (Daniel 9:24-27 and Luke 3:1,2)
A healer (Isaiah 35:5,6; Matthew 11:5)
Betrayed by a friend (Psalm 41:9 and John 13:18)
Betrayed for 30 pieces of silver (Zechariah 11:13 and Matthew 27:5-7)
Silver bought grave (Zechariah 11:13 and Matthew 27:5-7)
Death by crucifixion (Zechariah 12:10 and Matthew 27:31)
Executed with the wicked (Isaiah 53:9 and Matthew 27:38)
Given gall & vinegar to drink (Psalm 69:21 and Matthew 27:34)
Garments gambled away (Psalm 22:18 and Matthew 27:43)
Darkness at death (Zechariah 14:6 and Matthew 27:45)
Bones not broken (Psalm 34:20 and John 19:32f)
Earthquake at death (Zechariah 14:5 and Matthew 27:51)
Buried by the rich (Isaiah 53:96 and Matthew 27:57f)

SEE IN COLOR HERE:
http://bit.ly/JesusPredictions

Thank You

Thanks for reading my book! I'm so honored that you chose to spend your precious time with my research. You are appreciated. I'm an author who relies on my readers to help spread the word about stories you enjoy and facts you discover. Would you take a few minutes to let your friends know on Facebook, Pinterest... wherever you go online?

Also, each honest review on bookseller websites means a lot to me and helps other readers know if this is a book they might enjoy.

About The Author

Katheryn Maddox Haddad grew up in northern USA and now lives in India, where she doesn't have to shovel sunshine. She basks in 100-degree weather with banana trees, monkeys, and a computer with most of the letters worn off.

Besides the US and India, she has lived in four other countries ~ Korea, Canada, Afghanistan, and Abu Dhabi, and has made short visits to Tokyo and Sri Lanka.

With a bachelor's degree in English, Bible, and social science from Harding University and part of a master's degree in Bible from the Harding Graduate School of Theology (including Greek), she also has a master's degree in human relations from Abilene Christian University.

She spends half her day writing and the other half teaching English over the internet worldwide using the Bible as a textbook. She has taught nearly 10,000 Muslims over 15 years in the Middle East. Students she has converted to Christianity are in hiding in Afghanistan, Iran, Iraq, Yemen, Jordan, Uzbekistan, Tajikistan, and Palestine. "They are my heroes," she declares.

Currently, she also teaches Bible history at the MH School of Theology in Punadipadu, Krishna, Andhra Pradesh, India.

She is a member of American Christian Fiction Writers, the American Historical Association, World History Association, World Archaeological College, Association of Ancient Historians, and Archaeological Research Institute.

Oh, and for her next birthday, she plans to ride an elephant.

Coordinated With the Other Three Gospels

Connect With the Author

FACEBOOK

I welcome contact from readers, which you can do here:

Pictorial INDEX to all books & categories
Website: https://NorthernLightsPublishingHouse.com
Come read a sample chapter of each book

Facebook JUST ME Profile:
https://www.facebook.com/ReadsForAllAges/
Daily inspiration, poster, & prayer

Facebook BOOKS Page
https://www.facebook.com/katheryn.maddox.haddad/
Get in on weekly discounts only known by you

PINTEREST
https://www.pinterest.com/haddad1940/

YOUTUBE
https://www.youtube.com/@KH-bi3fr

email: khaddad1940@gmail.com

Matthew's Life of Christ

Buy Your Next Book Now

BIBLICAL HISTORICAL NOVELS
Series of 8: Soul Journey With the Real Jesus
Ongoing Series of 8: Intrepid Men of God

CHILDREN'S BIBLE STORYBOOKS
Series of 8: A Child's Life of Christ
Series of 10: A Child's Bible Heroes
Series of 8: A Child's Bible Kids

WORLDWIDE HISTORICAL RESEARCH
DOCUMENTARY, THESIS, NOVEL & SCREENPLAY WRITERS

BIBLE TOPICS
Applied Christianity: Handbook 500 Good Works
Christianity or Islam? The Contrast
The Holy Spirit: 592 Verses Examined
Inside the Hearts of Bible Women-Reader+Audio+Leader
Revelation: A Love Letter From God
Worship Changes Since 1st Century + Worship 1st Century Way
Was Jesus God? (Why Evil)
365 Life-Changing Scriptures Day by Date
The Road to Heaven
The Lord's Supper: 52 Readings with Prayers

BIBLE FUN BOOKS
Bible Puzzles, Bible Song Book, Bible Numbers

TOUCHING GOD SERIES
365 Golden Bible Thoughts: God's Heart to Yours
365 Pearls of Wisdom: God's Soul to Yours
365 Silver-Winged Prayers: Your Spirit to God's

SURVEY SERIES: EASY BIBLE WORKBOOKS
→Old Testament & New Testament Surveys
→Questions You Have Asked-Part I & II

Genealogy: How to Climb Your Family Tree Without Falling Out
Volume I & 2: Beginner-Intermediate & Colonial-Medieval

Genealogy: How to Climb Your Family Tree Without Falling Out
Volume I & 2: Beginner-Intermediate & Colonial-Medieval

www.ingramcontent.com/pod-product-compliance
Lightning Source LLC
Chambersburg PA
CBHW071324040426
42444CB00009B/2081